Contents

Don't be silly, Simon	4
Please leave the light on	20
Comparisons	22
The robot	24
Say what you mean! *A poem*	44
Riddles to share with spacemen and robots	46
Robot words	48

Don't be silly, Simon

"Time to get ready for the Book Week parade," said the teacher.

But Simon was looking out of the window. He had just seen a spaceship land in the playground.

"Hey, look, a spaceship," he said.

No one took any notice. They were too busy getting dressed up in their costumes. Even the teacher was too busy to listen.

Something small and strange got out of the spaceship. It looked just like the man from Mars in Simon's space book at home.

"Look, it's a man from Mars," he said.

Still no one took any notice.

"Come on, Simon, put your costume on," said the teacher. "We don't have all day."

"I saw a spaceship land in the playground," said Simon loudly, "and a man from Mars got out."

"Don't be silly, Simon," said the teacher. "It's someone dressed up. The big children are coming to the parade, too. Put your costume on right now, before I get cross."

Simon put on his cowboy costume.

"Hurry up," said the teacher, "I don't want my class to be last. Line up, now. It's time to go."

Simon looked over at the window. The strange little man was watching them through the glass.

"Look, it's the man from Mars," he said.

"Don't be silly, Simon," said the teacher. "Come along, children, and no talking!"

They went out into the playground. All the other classes were there and everyone was dressed up. There were witches and ghosts and rabbits and Goldilocks and the three bears and Superman and the three little pigs. Simon noticed that there were lots of cowboys, but he thought that his costume was the best. Nobody else had a gun like his.

Simon saw the man from Mars. He was watching the children line up.

"Into line," said a teacher.

She pushed the man from Mars in behind Simon.

"He's real," said Simon to the headteacher. "He came in a spaceship."

"Don't be silly, Simon," said the headteacher.

"Start walking," said a teacher and they all walked round and round and round while the headteacher and teachers looked at them.

Then the headteacher picked out one girl or boy from each class. They picked the man from Mars from Simon's class.

"That's not fair," said Simon. "He's real."

"Don't be silly, Simon," said his teacher.

Everyone sat down and watched while the children who had been picked walked round and round and round. Most of the children got tired of looking and started playing.
The cowboys were shooting at each other and the ghosts were trying to scare people and one of the bears made a little pig cry. But Simon didn't want to play. He was watching the man from Mars.

"I wonder what he will do," he thought.

Then the headteacher told everyone to stop playing and to sit down and listen to her. She said all the children who had been picked out would get a book.

"And the prize for the best costume," she said, "goes to the man from Mars."

All the teachers clapped and some of the children did, too.

"Come and get your prize," said the headteacher.

"That's not fair," said Simon. "He's real."

"Don't be silly, Simon," said his teacher.

She went over to the man from Mars.

"Go on, dear," she said.

But he took no notice. He didn't move. The teacher looked at him.

"I don't know who you are," she said. "Let's take your costume off, dear."

The man from Mars jumped away from her. Then he turned and ran across the playground to his spaceship. Some of the children ran after him.

"Look," they shouted. "It's a spaceship!"

"I told you there was a spaceship," said Simon. "I told you he was real."

Woosh! The spaceship took off.

"Wow! Look at it go!" everyone shouted.

"Oh, my goodness, he was real," said Simon's teacher.

"I told you he was," Simon said.

"Now who do we give the prize to?" said the headteacher. "Don't say we have to do it all over again."

"You could give it to me," said Simon.

"Don't be silly," said his teacher.

The TV people came to the school to find out about the man from Mars. They didn't want to talk to the headteacher and they didn't want to talk to any of the teachers. They wanted to talk to Simon.

"I told them he was real," Simon said. "I told them lots of times."

And this time, everyone listened.

Please leave the light on

Please leave the light on tonight, Mum.
It's not that I'm scared, you know.
It's just that I can't help thinking
about that TV show.
The one where the witch came riding
out of the dark night sky
and grabbed that girl from out of her bed
before she could blink an eye.
Then she took her away to a house in the woods
where she lived with three black cats
and shut her up in a little room
that was full of mean old rats.
So please leave the light on tonight, Mum.
It's not that I'm scared, you know.
It's just that I can't help thinking
about that TV show.
And I don't know if she got away,
I was too scared to watch, you see.
For I suddenly thought
that one of these nights a witch
might come looking for
        ME!

Pat Edwards

The robot

It was a week before Christmas.
Dad came home with a big box.
"What is it?" Caroline asked him.

"Wait and see," said Dad laughing.

"Can't we open it now?" asked James.

"No, it's for Christmas," said Mum.
"It's a surprise for the two of you."

Mum and Dad put the box by the Christmas tree. There were lots of other things under the tree, but the box was the biggest one of them all.
"You'll never guess what it is," laughed Mum.

The day before Christmas, Caroline looked at the box again.
"What do you think it is?" she asked James.

"I don't know," James answered.
He tried to pick the box up but he couldn't.
Then Caroline tried to look into the box.
But she couldn't see anything at all.

Christmas morning came and Dad said to them, "NOW you can open the box!"

"Good! Let me do it," said James.

"No, that's not right. Let me!" said Caroline.

"Open it together," said Mum.
The two children pulled the lid off the box.
It was full of pieces of metal and lots of other things.

"What is it?" asked James.

"What is it?" asked Caroline.

"It's a robot," said Dad.

"But it's just pieces of metal and things," said James.

"Ah," said Dad. "You have to put it together yourselves. That will keep the two of you quiet all through Christmas!"

There was a book in the box, too.
James and Caroline looked at it.
It told them how to make the robot.
It told them where to put the metal pieces and how to put all the other things together.

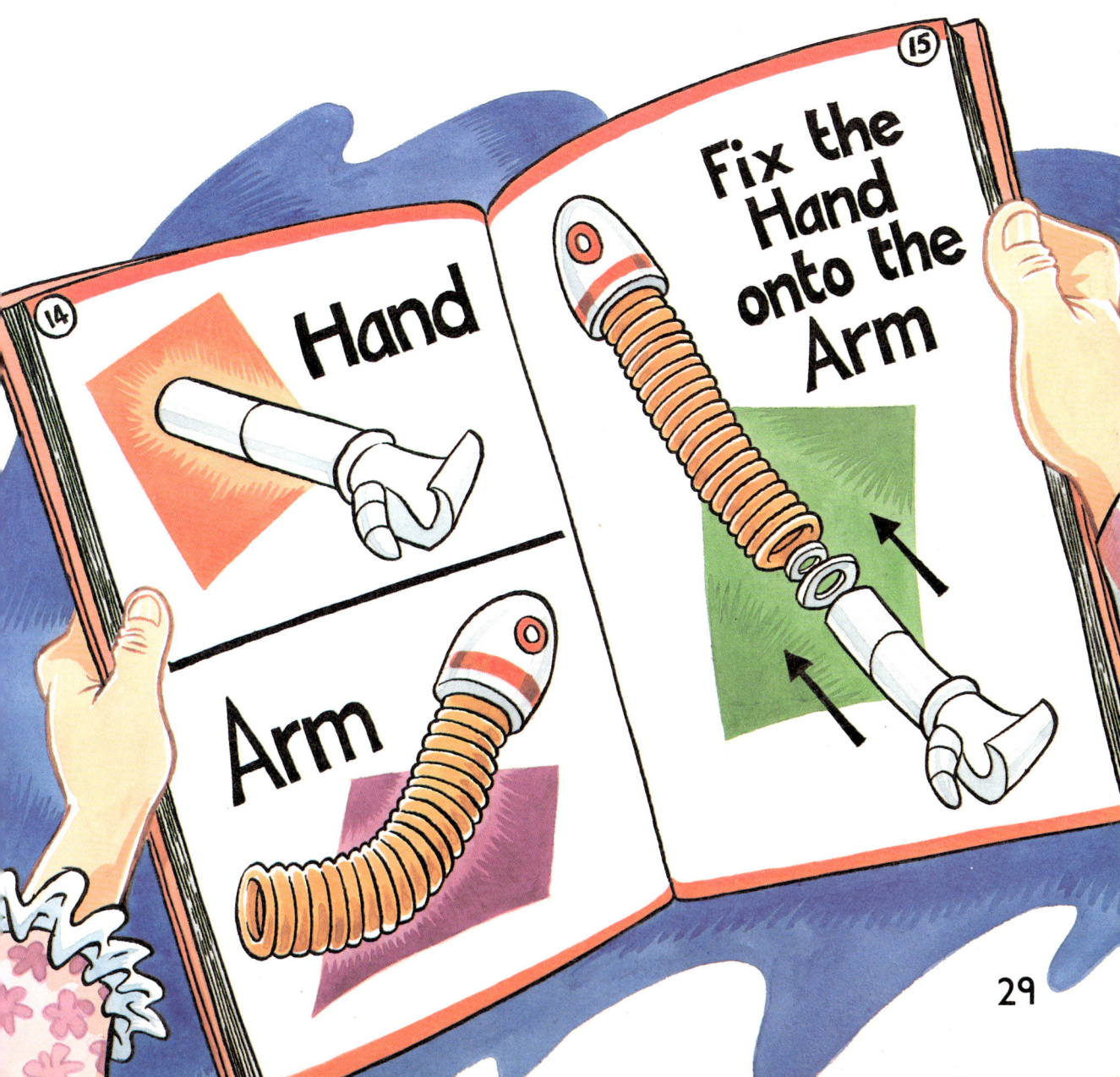

At the end of the week, the robot was made. "But will it work?" asked Caroline.

"The book said we just have to tell the robot what to do," answered James.

"OK. Robot, walk!" said Caroline. The robot walked down the room.

"Robot, stop!" said James. The robot stopped.

"Robot, sit!" said Caroline. The robot sat.

"It works! We've made it work!" shouted Caroline.

"Now we can get it to do things around the house, like it tells you in the book," said James.

"This is going to be fun," said Caroline.
"Let me have first go."

"Robot, do the washing up!" said Caroline.
What do you think the robot did?
It went into the kitchen, but it did not
go to the sink. It went to the washing basket.
It picked up the washing and threw it up in the air.
There was washing all over the place!

"Let's try again," said James.
"Robot, draw the curtains!"
What do you think the robot did?
It went over to the table and picked up
a felt pen. Then it **drew** a picture of
curtains all over the wall!
"Oh no," said James. "Look what it's done."

"Let's try again," said Caroline.
"Robot, dust the room!"
What do you think the robot did?
It went over to the vacuum cleaner.
Then the robot took the dust bag out of the
vacuum cleaner and threw dust all over the room!
"Oh no," said Caroline. "Now look what it's done."

"Let's try again," said James.
"Robot, make the bed!"
What do you think the robot did?
It went upstairs.
"Good," said James.
Then the robot came down again.
It went into the shed and there was a lot of banging.
Then it came out with a bed that it had made!

"Perhaps it can only do simple things,"
said Caroline. "I know . . . Robot, open the door!"
What do you think the robot did?
It went over to the door. It pulled the front off
the door. It pulled the back off the door.
And then it tried to look inside it!
"Oh no," said Caroline. "Look what it's done."

"Let me try something simple," said James.
"Robot, make a cup of tea!"
What do you think the robot did?
It went to the cupboard and took out a cup.
Then it got out the tea bags.
"Good," said James, "it's getting it right."
But the robot pushed tea bags into the cup until it was full!
"Oh no," said James.

"There must be SOMETHING it can do," said Caroline.
"Robot, clean my shoes!"
What do you think the robot did?
It made Caroline sit down and then it took off her shoes.
"Good," said Caroline.
But the robot took the shoes into the kitchen and threw them into the washing machine!

"We'll give it one more try," said James.
"Robot, switch on the TV."
What do you think the robot did?
It went to the television and then it went to the wall.
It pulled the light switch off the wall and put it
on the television!
"That is the end!" said James.

They looked at all the mess the robot had made.
"That's it," said Caroline. "Whatever will Mum and Dad say when they come in?"

"We must clean it all up before they see it," said James. But it was too late.
In came Mum and Dad.

"What a mess!" said Mum.

"What have you been doing?" asked Dad.

"It's the robot," said Caroline.

"It can't do anything right," said James.
"It's a silly robot, it's no use at all."

"Let me try," said Mum. "Robot lay the table!"
What do you think the robot did?
It went over to the table.
"There you are," said Mum.

But the robot picked up the table and turned it upside down on the floor!
"There you are," said James.

42

"Right," said Dad. "Back it goes to the shop."

"Wait," said Caroline, "Robot, back in the box!"
What do you think the robot did?
It went back in the box!
It was the only thing it had done right all day!

Say what you mean!

I'm the robot that was built
by James and Caroline,
they think I've got a problem
but the problem isn't mine!

They built me very carefully
(from instructions in the book)
and if they think I do things wrong,
they should take another look.

I do the things they tell me to
(I'm really pretty snappy)
but somehow when I've finished,
they don't look very happy!

"Robot," they say, "do this, do that,"
(and it doesn't take me long)
but then they end up cross with me –
they say I've got it wrong!

I only do just what they say
(that's what words mean to me),
I can't help it if they won't
speak plainly – don't you see?

Wendy Body

Riddles to share with spacemen and robots

When can't spacemen land on the moon?

When it's full.

What laughs and goes to the moon?

A space chuckle.

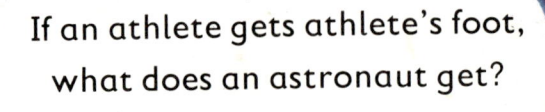

If an athlete gets athlete's foot, what does an astronaut get?

Missile toe.

What did the astronaut see in the frying pan?

An unidentified frying object.

Where do spacemen leave their spaceships?

At parking meteors.

Which robot wears the biggest hat?

The one with the biggest head.

When do robots have four legs?

When there are two of them.

Robot words

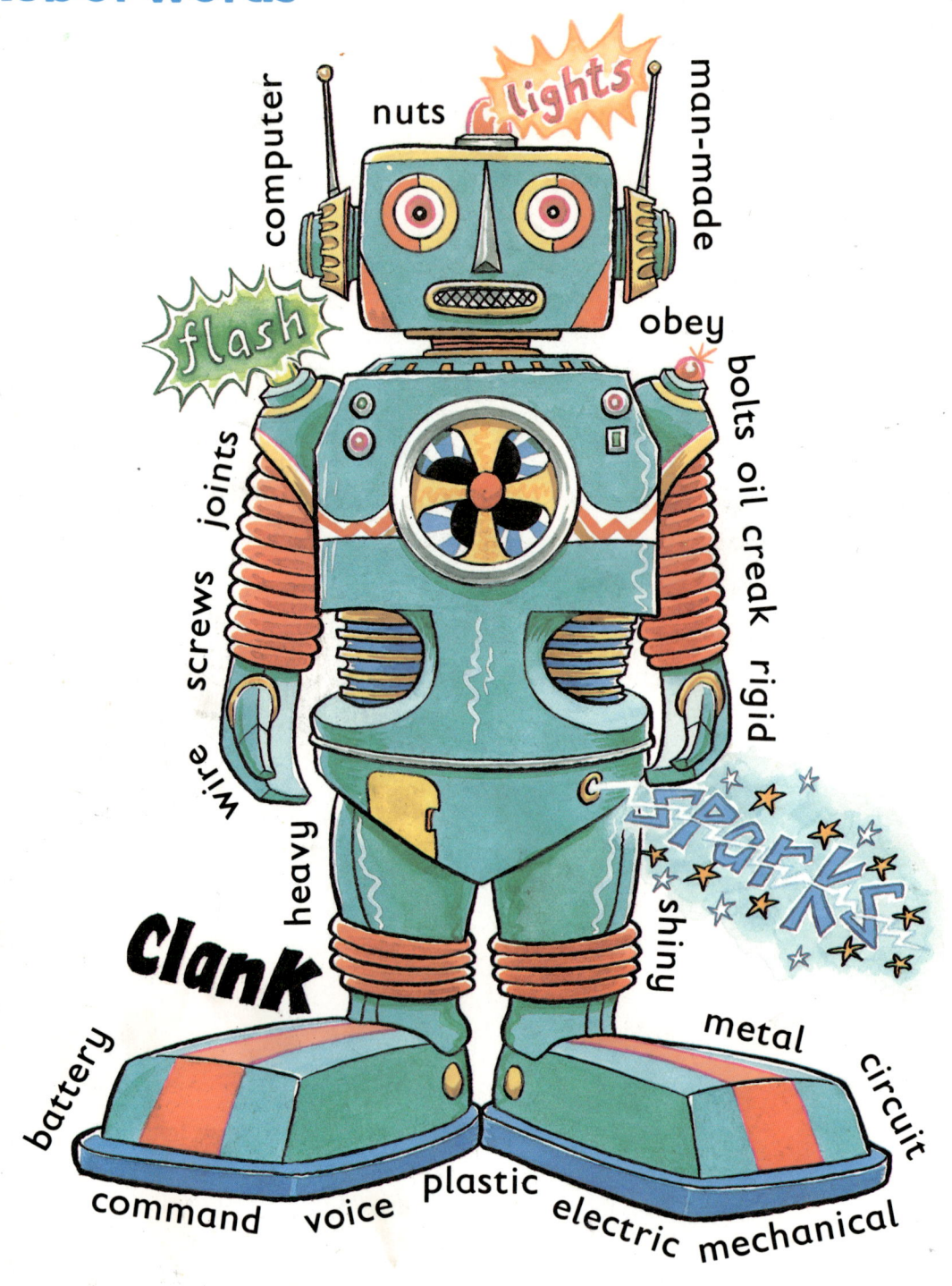

computer, nuts, lights, man-made, flash, obey, bolts, oil, creak, rigid, joints, screws, wire, heavy, Clank, shiny, sparks, battery, command, voice, plastic, electric, metal, mechanical, circuit